Silly Old] Look for Treasure

written by Jay Dale
illustrated by Nick Diggory

Two silly old pirates
walked along the beach.

"Oh, where, oh, where
is the hidden treasure?"
said the little pirate with the big hat.
"We have been looking all day."

"Yes," said the big pirate
with the little hat.
"We have been looking all day long."

"Look!" said the little pirate.
"Here is a treasure map.
Our captain has left it behind."

"This map will help us to find the hidden treasure," smiled the big pirate.

So the two silly old pirates looked at the map.

First they ran quickly along the beach.
Then they hopped over six black rocks.
Next they walked across an old log.
At last, they came to a big cave.

"Oh!" said the little pirate.
"I can see a big cave.
The treasure will be in this cave."

"Yes," smiled the big pirate.
"The treasure will be in this cave.
Let's go!"

So the two silly old pirates ran quickly inside.

"Look!" shouted the little pirate. "There is a box behind the rocks. Maybe the treasure is hidden in this box."

"Yes," smiled the big pirate. "Maybe it is!"

So the two silly old pirates opened the lid.

Creak!

"Oh!" said the little pirate.
"I am so sad.
There is **no** treasure in the box."
And with that, he began to cry.
"Boo-hoo! Boo-hoo!"

"Look!" said the big pirate.
"I can see some paper in the box.
Maybe it is a new treasure map."

The paper said ...

Dear Silly Old Pirates

You were too slow!

I got here first.

The treasure is all for me!

From your captain

And with that, the two silly old pirates cried and cried.
"Boo-hoo! Boo-hoo!"